Milestone 70

Carol Murphy

Pendle Hill Pamphlet 287

Request for permission to quote or to translate should be addressed to Pendle Hill Publications, Wallingford, PA 19086.

Copyright © 1989 by Pendle Hill

ISBN 0-87574-287-4

Library of Congress Catalog card number 89-061817

September 1989: 2,500

The only child of a poet father and a musician mother, I grew up a bookish youngster with few playmates. My abilities ran in the groove of reading, thinking and observing rather than participating. This work, with all its virtues and limitations, became my vocation. The milestone of seventy years focused that vocation as I paused to look at the tenor of my days in that seventy-first year.

December 7 ▪ Today I "cracked" a new book I bought for myself: a biography of Alan Watts by the English writer Monica Furlong, whose life of Thomas Merton I also own. She is sensitive both to religion and psychology. I have enjoyed many of Watts' writings, but found his revealingly titled memoirs *In My Own Way*, egotistic though charming. How could a Buddhist non-believer in the self have so much ego? Furlong explains him as a "trickster" type—like the trickster gods of mythology who are often naughty but achieve some good for humanity anyway. The Indians' coyote trickster brought fire to humankind, as Prometheus did, but got his tail scorched in so doing.

Possibly the philosophical denial of self is a cover-up for egoism. More realistically we all feel "lonely and afraid in a world we never made;" self is psychologically real and self-defenses always creep into our responses. The best we can do is to be aware of this ego-awareness and discount it as possible. Only the saints can go further.

December 9 ▪ A rainy day, good for writing Christmas letters. I have fewer on my list every year, but I still correspond with a woman a few years older than myself, whom I met through my writings. She had read one of my pamphlets and wrote to ask for some spiritual guidance. She felt isolated in a rural area, and had a constant concern for a child with learning disabilities, and she wanted spiritual and psychological growth. There was little I could do but exchange sympathetic comments and give her the name of a religiously oriented counselor. This led her into other relationships, and into the field of guidance counseling, from which she has now retired. For me, the relationship has brought a comfortable mix of sharing thoughts with geographical distance. We have exchanged visits over the years, but are otherwise content to be epistolary.

In relationships, I think, the need for emotional support varies. Possibly it's the same, in my case, with various interests I have pursued. I don't seem to fall in love with people so much as with such pursuits as birdwatching or t'ai-chi, which became temporary vehicles for some value or latent ability which I needed to enrich my life.

December 16 ▪ I watched the movie *Yentl* on TV last night. More than a glimpse of old-time *shtetl* life and a series of androgynous episodes which defy our usual sexual boundary lines, *Yentl* is a meditation on the intellectual woman as displaced person. The seriously intellectual or artistic woman is still a marginal person. If Yentl had been a Catholic, she might have become a nun and founded a teaching order. Protestants and Jews have less well-charted paths. Mine is that of a Quaker celibate, not unprecedented, but still marginal in my very married and suburban Meeting.

December 18 ▪ On sampling a collection of Isaac Bashevis Singer's stories, I'm interested to note that he has touched on androgynous themes in at least two stories. In one story, a transvestite youth elopes from his arranged marriage to live as the "wife" of a male friend of his until a sudden outburst of heterosexual passion for a girl leads to his accidental death. In another story a saintly young Hasid develops his capacity for androgyny, and has a marriage ceremony for his *animus* aspect to wed his female or *anima* aspect. Are these playful blurrings of biological sex symbolic of a deep questioning of over-rigid sex roles? (Compare also the recent movies *Tootsie* and *Victor/Victoria*.)

In my own case, thank God, my father was never *macho*—a gentle poet indifferent to sports or hunting, and my mother was a musician who hated housework. I was free to become a Yentl.

Christmas Day ▪ Nowadays we think of time as linear, but on special occasions we experience it as circular. Between Christmasses, we forget the feeling of the last Christmas. Then the act of getting out the decorations from storage takes us right back to the time when we last put them away; Christmas decorations have to be aged to be legitimate. Christmas links to Christmas, and the intervening time falls away. But not for always; old Christmas-times do recede. There were the stiff, over-stuffed Christmasses with grandmother, the awakening as a child to see the bumpy shape of a stuffed stocking at the foot of my bed, the Christmas when my mother was in the hospital, eerily echoed, eleven years later and a few years ago when I was in the same hospital a few days before Christmas, when what sounded like the same amateur carolers were singing off-key in the corridors.

December 27 ▪ Paging through a wealth of pictures in a book called *The Library in America* led me to recall with gratitude my experiences with libraries in the past, from the miniature rotunda of the sturdy little Carnegie library in Rockport, Massachusetts, to the great, echoing rotunda of the Library of Congress. The first library fed my childish mind and the second served up the books I needed for my graduate work in international relations. Libraries have been life-savers for my mother and me during lonely war years in Washington and Philadelphia. They furnished not only food for thought but a succession of good mystery stories for reading aloud. Before the days of TV, reading aloud was always our evening diversion. I am grateful for special "finds" in some of these libraries: in Gloucester, Massachusetts, I came across a copy of Thomas Kelly's *Testament of Devotion*, which spoke to the condition of my early religious search. I also like to recall an afternoon spent in the library at Carmel, California, where a fire burned cozily in a fieldstone fireplace.

December 28 ▪ I finished reading a life of Teilhard de Chardin today. A strange thought—of resemblances between Teilhard and Alan Watts, otherwise very different from each other: one a devoted Catholic, the other the playboy of Western Zen. Yet both died suddenly at a time when they felt their lives no longer had anywhere to go, and both leaned rather heavily on relationships with devoted women who arranged the practical sides of their lives. It's hard not to find a certain egotism in the use of these women as the men press onward and upward to some abstract vision. And there is something that tempts women to such subservience. Yet does one want to adopt the "my fulfillment first" attitude of today?

December 29 ▪ I have been reading some of May Sarton's journals. It was Elizabeth Vining's and May Sarton's idea of making special records of their seventieth year that gave me the idea of doing likewise, as a follower, not an imitator.

Sarton quotes Bernard Berenson as saying, "I have had the dream of life lived as a sacrament." I've recently reviewed a manuscript by a Lutheran on the place of liturgy and sacrament in worship, comparing Lutheran with Quaker practice. Here is a subject which goes to the heart of the relationship between form and substance in religion. I must acknowledge that I'm not personally touched by ritual. Perhaps this is because when I was an impressionable child, my parents were ex-Catholics not yet Quakers, having no observances apart from their quiet lives of poetry and music. Rituals have to begin in childhood, a naturally ritualistic age, to speak to the deep unconscious beyond the level of conscious beliefs and they can be later returned to as a kind of home base after one's youthful religious revolt has run its course. I remain something of an outsider, and my religious awareness is not summoned by deliberate attempts at coming into the presence of the holy; it must creep up on me unawares.

I observe in the seemingly secular world the survival of certain rituals, only overtly non-religious. For example, the "housing" of a new fire engine at our local firehouse, when the new truck must be pushed by hand into the house three times— once for God, once for country and once for the firefighters. But, as it should be, what began with solemnity ended with laughter, beer and hot dogs. Rituals and festivals come close together. Sports like baseball can be ritualistic, too; the national anthem, the drama of skill, and the ukases of the umpires. Baseball is its own universe with its own "sacred" history.

January 1, 1987 ▪ As with Christmas, the coming of a new year cycles back to memories of previous years. I remember, before the war, driving around the streets of Washington, honking along with other drivers at the midnight hour. More recently, there were times of combined worship and friendly celebration at Pendle Hill. Here where I now live, there have been nights when the folks downstairs have loudly partied with blaring rock music till the dawn. There have been minor disasters, as when some boys next door launched a whistling rocket through one of my windows, alarming the whole household.

Thinking back over the past year, I count pluses and minuses. Having participated in a workshop for Friends meeting librarians, I have climbed a rung in the ladder of capability. A year or so ago I was in a state of dismay at having a library, as someone has said, "dumped in my lap." Now I am much more empowered. On the minus side, my two remaining aunts died within months of each other. They were not very close to me; one was an eccentric who was good at alienating everybody, and the other a docile mental retardate living in a Catholic rest home. They are at peace now; but during the past year they were both in and out of hospitals and nursing homes, the occasion of many emergency telephone calls and an occasional journey of two hundred miles through New York area traffic. I still over-react to the ringing of the telephone.

Like many my age and older, I give thought to eventual sheltered living for myself. Some people I know have moved to a life-care retirement center. I have visited one; it's beautiful and luxurious (by my simple standards), and also isolated, like a grand cruise ship, completely self-sufficient and isolated from the former activities and connections of its passengers, from which there is no landing save a garden cemetery. I'm not ready for such a drastic cutting of my few ties to a real community.

This afternoon I'm keeping my ties in order by going to a friend's open house. Many of my fellow meeting members will be there, and I will marvel at their ability for social chatter and consumption of canapes while I will stand balancing a cup mostly in silence. For one thing, I have no accomplished grandchildren or exciting foreign cruises to chat about.

January 2 ▪ A wet and stormy day, good for dismantling the little Christmas tree built of styrofoam balls stuck with toothpicks. I reviewed the cards I received, including a belated note from an old schoolmate I hadn't heard from in years.

That evening I relaxed with glorious Handel and Bach music on PBS and a tour of King's College Chapel in Cambridge.

January 11 ▪ I have been reading May Sarton's *World of Light*: vivid descriptions of her parents and many of her wonderful friends. Friends, too, play a part in her recent novel, *The Magnificent Spinster*. Its central point is the validity of a life of many friendships but no marriage. I'm afraid many men readers will become tired of the gentle endearments of the feminine conversation amid flower pieces and fine old furniture. It's a relief to read of genuinely kind people in an unkind and lonely world, yet one perversely wishes for a touch of vinegar in this blandness.

There is similar lovingkindness in Daisy Newman's *A Golden String*, which relates the genesis of the idealized Rhode Island Quakers of her novels. Friends (small "f") have played a large part in Daisy Newman's life. It made me realize how comparatively friendless my parents were. Wholly unworldly, they huddled in out-of-season resort towns, living on a small inheritance rather than looking for contacts that would connect them with the intelligentsia to which they should have belonged. So used was I to a reclusive way of life that it took conscious and belated effort to break away to join the Pendle Hill community.

January 15 ▪ Sometimes an endearing little incident comes along to mitigate the dreariness of a train-ride into town. One time it was the sight of a cindery plot of wasteland beside the tracks blued over by a growth of chicory in bloom. Today it was the irreverent humor of a trainman on the way home. The train was delayed and bumped along in a desultory way. Over the loudspeaker a voice explained "the less than relentless pace" of the train as due to something wrong with the rear cars and ended: "Thank you for your patience, ladies and gentlemen, and please include SEPTA in your prayers." We all relaxed with a good laugh at our wayward transit system.

January 18 ▪ A day of sleet and rain. I'm glad I braved the weather to go to meeting for I can now add another to a list of "authentic" persons or endeavors motivated by a religious faith which is not dogma, but by a spirit of love and dedication articulated in action, yet different from the drive of a purely secular reformer. An example is Mother Teresa, a sentimental favorite of many; but seen at length in a PBS documentary is more than a glorified nurse. She asks no one to imitate her unless called to the same all-sacrificing devotion and she concentrates on the service she does best.

The spirit behind the AFSC at its best, at least as articulated by Asia Bennett recently, tries to balance the awareness of the structural reforms needed in a world of wide-spread injustices, with a quiet spirit of loving care, which must always be the wellspring of reform and "do-gooding."

Today, Steve Angell of the FCNL spoke at our forum. Here again was someone occupied in Congress-watching and lobbying, but in-spirited by a deep faith in the power of God to take away all occasion for wars.

So often there tends to be a split between spirituality and activism. I have known Friends who worry endlessly about the world's woes and others who worry endlessly about the minutiae of Quaker worship or repeating well-worn religious phrases. But every now and then one meets these "authentic" people. Another one, not in public life, is a fellow-writer, a poet and peace-activist, whose quiet English voice, reading her simple but contemplative poems always impresses her hearers.

January 30 ▪ On this gloomy, snow-covered day it was good to hear a familiar mewing call and spot a yellow-bellied sapsucker in the maple tree. Daily bird-watching is a habit that has somehow fallen away, partly from other preoccupations and partly because of the great diminution of local species. There are now mockingbirds and house finches (fairly recent comers), but a decrease of the warblers, the varieties of sparrows and thrushes that used to come in their appointed seasons. Then there was Tinicum Marsh, now hardly attainable through a tangle of airport and I-95 traffic, where I used to be able to see black terns, cattle egrets, ruffs, buff-breasted sandpipers and as many as ten thousand pintails. Now, alas, the effort is hardly that rewarding. Still I haven't lost my eye and ear for a bird in passing.

February 8 ▪ In meeting this morning I thought of a new area of psyche to add to Freud's id, ego and superego. The trouble with the ego-self and its armor, the persona, is that it is always ambivalent—dependent on others for approval and vulnerable to disapproval and rejection. Often these come from the same person, especially parents and siblings, hence the love-hate relationship that sours all human relationships. The superego participates in this as the internalized approval/disapproval of the bearers of the cultural norms. I propose the fourth area would be the "meta-ego" or "extra-ego"—that which directs the person away from self-consciousness or satisfaction of needs, whether of id or ego. The esthetic sense of beauty, absorption in creation, or meditative mysticism are instances of this. The Inward Light of the Quakers would find ingress in this part of the psyche.

February 18 ▪ A senior citizen group I've recently joined is starting to discuss Isak Dinesen's stories. Dreamlike and archetypal, they seem to bewilder the relentlessly factual minds of this conventional and middle-class group. What a contrast to the Jungian-minded religion and psychology conferences I have attended, where fairy-tale archetypes are more real than everyday life. Compared to them, I am boringly rationalistic; but here, in this senior group, I tend to plead for the recognition of a truth not communicated by "facts" alone.

When I read "New Age" literature, I am bemused by its cloudy inspirationalism. Somehow it never connects with earth. It's then I turn for relief to the facts and figures mentality of scientists and engineers, only to miss the sense of the reality of the non-measurable.

March 11 ▪ A new Papal pronouncement on the sinfulness of artificial insemination and fertilization set me to thinking of how traditional religion is still often ruled by fear of the increasing power of humankind to manage our biological fate. To be sure, we need to be reminded that such power can be used for evil as well as good, that technology does not equal progress. But Christianity should surely be on the side of love that cuts out fear, that dedicates our abilities to carrying on the upward thrust of God's creative Spirit by conscious means. Instead, religious authorities fall back into a kind of pantheism that identifies nature's involuntary happenings with the will of God.

I am prepared to be more of a "pantheist" than are many nonmystical theologians, but not to go to the extreme of identifying either procreation or disease with the will of God.

We do have to understand and cooperate with nature to guide it to a higher purpose; and it does seem that we often tend to cut across nature's grain with willful and impatient interventions that raise nearly unanswerable questions of parentage, as with surrogate motherhood, for example. Feminists would say this is a typically *macho* approach, akin to the doctors who use Caesarians when natural childbirth would do as well. Here is where a church open to feminine understanding would be a better guide than negative pronouncements by celibate patriarchs.

March 12 ▪ In a radio interview, a Vietnam veteran related his experiences as an officer in combat. He told how the troops were trained to depersonalize the enemy by calling them "gooks" to make killing them psychologically possible. He also said he felt he had no right to pass a moral judgment on this; he was merely following his government's orders. Here was a thoroughly decent man, capable of brotherly love for his fellow vets, speaking like a "good German."

Anti-war activists should uphold two vital resolutions: one never depersonalize any person or group of persons, and two, never abdicate one's right of moral judgment to anyone else—least of all to a government. Much more needs to be done to weaken the war system, but these two are basic.

As a kind of footnote to this subject of depersonalization, I recalled the Friend who recently in meeting confessed her inability to feel Christian love for Hitler. A day or two later I read an article in *Friends Journal* whose author found compassion for the unloved child Hitler had been. Then yesterday the seniors' discussion group considered Flannery O'Connor's story "A Good Man is Hard to Find," in which the old grandmother, about to be killed, has a moment of grace when she felt her murderer could have been one of her own children. The "Misfit," as the murderer called himself, was not quite able to accept that absolution, and many people will see such moments as impotent sentimentality; nevertheless, it is for Flannery O'Connor a glimpse into the power of Christ, who forgives us, for we know not what we do.

March 15 ▪ When people ask me, "What are you writing now?" I am embarrassed to try to answer. I wish at these times that I could present the picture of an industrious writer dedicating the morning hours to work at a word processor. But I don't. It takes me several years to have enough ideas to work with and the result is put down in longhand at odd moments. Thinking time and reading are part of my work, not the leisure-time activities they may be to others.

Yet often my days become cluttered enough with details. It has been said that the trouble with women scholars is that they don't have wives. Certainly I could use a helpful other to defrost the fridge, gather the laundry, service the car and pay the bills on time.

On a more serious note, I've been watching a visual essay on the art of the Wyeth family by Charles Kuralt. Many people look down on realistic art, but I admire the deeply loving, almost religious feeling of Andrew and James Wyeth for what Wordsworth called:

The unassuming things that hold

A silent station in this beauteous world.

Here is no Warhol soup-can, but plain farm animals and implements that reach to the holiness described by Zechariah when "every pot in Jerusalem and Judah shall be sacred to the Lord of Hosts." Andrew Wyeth told Kuralt that he wasn't made to go to church on Sundays, but found his religion in soaking in the lay of his homeland.

Ironically, at this point I had to turn off the TV to go to meeting. I, too, am often tempted, with Emily Dickinson, to keep the Sabbath by staying at home, "with a bobolink for a chorister, And an orchard for a dome." Yet there is a need for sharing with others even if only in Whittier's "silence multiplied by the still forms on either side."

March 20 ▪ I have been mulling over the rift that seems to be opening up between two kinds of Quaker committee members. This was pointed out at yesterday's Book Services meeting. Most are elderly ladies—and a few men—who are able to come to day-time meetings but not in the evenings. The younger people who should be taking over our tasks are at work all day and could come only in the evening. And working parents with children find it hard to come at any time. The Quaker structure has been built on the existence of leisure time, or a willingness, like John Woolman, to curtail attention to business affairs in order to do the Society's work. Must we devise a way of compensating people for taking a day away from work, as are jurors in court trials? Is our yuppie culture too frenetic for religious endeavor to survive?

March 24 ▪ I'm reading Margaret Hope Bacon's new life of Henry Cadbury. He is the very model of a nonmystical Quaker, excelling in two other directions not always found together—the scholarly and the activist. His religious life had to be that of the steward working in the absence of this Lord. I would agree that Jesus spoke to the needs of the nonmystic and that we cannot confine the religious life to contemplatives only, otherwise I as well as Cadbury would be outside the pale. I believe, nevertheless, religion derives its life from those who immediately apprehend a reality that is more than our daily secular state of mind. If I hadn't steeped myself in the mystics, I would never have hungered for this deeper reality nor thought it credible. In Cadbury's case, his family's Quaker tradition was fixed in his unconscious. However he might question it, it was Quakerism and the Gospels which drew his scholarly abilities. Many of us live to some extent as second-hand parasites of the contemplative tradition.

As a matter of practical guidance, Cadbury and I belong among those I call "buses" rather than "trolleys." The mystical "trolley" is always in contact with guiding rail and empowering wire, while the nonmystical "bus" is self-powered and self-steering. But you have to have some sort of plan or compass to indicate your destination. Something in us must point to true North.

March 27 ▪ Yearly Meeting time again. It's hard to believe I've attended about ten since becoming a more active Friend. Again, as at Christmas, time coils in a circle and each occasion hooks up with last year's. Some of the faces change, some have vanished forever, but the great West Room, the clogged meal lines, the earnest and high-minded exhortations are much the same. At times it's inspiring, but I now tend to have a sense of *déjà vu*. Much the same things are said every year. Minutes are proposed, nearly approved, then fall before the nitpicking of those who wish to assert themselves; though some indeed have a valid "stop" in the mind. A few, like Winifred Rawlins, contribute a voice of sanity and real centeredness to the discussions.

April 12 ▪ Our meeting fell into one of its periodic and frustrating debates about a frequent troublesome visitor to our worship. The same arguments were voiced that I've heard—and contributed to—for the last ten years. It now became apparent to me that we are trying to use either rational argument or moral reproach to influence someone who is mentally disturbed at a deeper level than reason or moral finger-pointing can reach. One can imagine that a deeply spiritual person could touch this deepest level; short of that, there is the basic physical level of the medication which this person should be taking and sometimes doesn't. But we are neither saints nor psychiatrists; hence our helplessness is manifest. Is this perhaps the weakness of us middle-class liberals in the face of the mass insecurity, of cruelty and war? We reason, we scold, and nothing seems to happen.

April 21 ▪ I now have undertaken a new task: as I age I un-retire! This task is sending birthday cards on behalf of the meeting to members seventy-five years of age or older. Most of the names are new to me; a few I know, and some of these are still very active in meeting affairs, younger people being too busy and exhausted to take on these matters.

I remember my mother receiving such cards from someone in the meeting who didn't know her or follow up with inquiries; my mother felt rather ironic about this formal gesture. Basically, a meeting has to reach those who congenially share a common interest in spiritual search and expression, beyond ordinary sociability. Well, we'll see what comes of this card-sending and whether it can go beneath the surface.

April 27 ▪ Not all of TV is trivial entertainment. Last night I saw the play "Pack of Lies" on the Hallmark Hall of Fame. On the surface it could be taken as a spy thriller: were the mysterious secret service man who watched them from next door the real villain? But it became more and more clear that a disturbing ethical dilemma was being explored. There is the question posed by E.M. Forster's saying he would betray his country for a friend. Is the country a mere abstraction or is it all of us protecting our social cohesion? At any rate, the practice of spying and counter-spying destroys mutual faith and trust. This is the real evil of the sin of lying: it poisons the core of human relationships. Yet total frankness can be disruptive also. What is the relationship between reticence and truthfulness? There is much to meditate about here.

It seems rather melodramatic for the play to end with the report of the main character's decline and death as the aftermath; it might have been more artistic to have ended with her daughter Julie's confrontation with the imprisoned neighbor— the latter unforgiving of what she saw as betrayal, the former silently accusing her of false friendship. But the report of the death at least makes the point that you destroy a person when you destroy her deepest relationship.

April 28 ▪ A fiftieth college reunion yearbook arrived today—the brief autobiographies of my classmates, most of whom I hardly knew, since I was a day student at college. I enjoyed the give and take of seminar discussions, but my extracurricular life took place at home, where we maintained as much as possible our family activities of quiet study and reading aloud in the evening. The more extrovert students seemed lightweight to me then. Now, as I peruse these biographies, I'm in awe of their multitudinous accomplishments. We have one Nobel laureate and at least one retired college president, two Rhodes scholars and many who have a slew of grandchildren and several vacation homes. I remain a little gray church mouse. In reading, I've found personal differences similar to those I saw in other compilations, such as one of my father's '07 Harvard class. There are the chatty "Hi fellas, life has been wonderful" entries, the inhibited, bare listing of positions held and dates, and the chamber-of-commerce-style resume of civic good deeds. Also a few of the artistic, wryly odd-ball characters at the other end of the spectrum from the "squares." Measured by this scale, I suppose my contribution is somewhere in the middle—both odd-ball and somewhat "square."

Finally, I'm surprised and pleased that so many of us septuagenarians are still active. The same is true of the over-seventy-fives on my birthday list. Those who survive the auto accidents of youth and coronaries of middle age are truly tough!

Later that evening, I watched part of the series *Shoah* on PBS—memories of the Holocaust of the Jews—and then watched a more peaceful journey to Pennsylvania's Endless Mountain country. A contrast? Perhaps not. In both programs one saw vistas of logging roads through young forest, village church steeples pointing to the sky, while country people with weathered faces did their chores. There were no old ovens for burning Jews in Pennsylvania, though perhaps a few dead Indians mouldered under the fields; but wouldn't these farmers display the same blunting of compassion if some unwelcome minority were to be seized in their backyards? Most of us are nice while our lives are nice; but when under threat we can readily turn mean. Poles or Americans, we are all under judgment. Who should cast the first stone?

May 8 ▪ This has been a week of unsavory political revelations, giving rise to more reflections on the nature of sinfulness.

On Capitol Hill, Richard Secord has been unveiling the complicated web of intrigue in the Iran/Contra affair. It is said that Ronald Reagan loved to listen to the CIA's William Casey tell his stories of undercover exploits; a reminder that the apparently folksy and non-aggressive are fascinated by the dark and unscrupulous. It is there they find their buried shadow side and become vulnerable to it. Othello and Iago are symbiotic. To take a metaphor from Isak Dinesen, they are two caskets, the key of each being locked in the other.

Hence the religious teaching that we must deal with our own evil before riding forth to do battle with other "evil empires." Recommended reading: Ursula Le Guin's *The Wizard of Earthsea*, in which the hero, having loosed evil into the world, must call it by his own name before it can be overcome.

May 22 ▪ I'm reading Doris Kearns Goodwin's capacious account of the Fitzgerald and Kennedy families—the road from "Honey Fitz" to "Camelot." I noted with interest that Rose Fitzgerald, now the Kennedy matriarch, was to enter Wellesley College about the time my mother was there, and Joe Kennedy went to Harvard a few years after my father did. These were the days of Emily Green Balch and Vida Scudder at Wellesley and of Santayana and William James at Harvard. My mother learned to appreciate the wider freedom of thought at Wellesley. My father must surely have noted the social limitation at Harvard of being named Murphy, but he seemed never to have looked for social acceptance, as Joe Kennedy did. He was content with playing chess, studying poetry and philosophy and visiting my mother at Wellesley.

Both my mother and father quietly dropped the dogmatic side of their rather fitfully Catholic upbringing, while retaining its poetical and mystical element, to remain unchurched until a growing interest in Quaker writings brought them into the Society of Friends.

May 24 ▪ At Quarterly Meeting, we had a pep talk and video tape of an inner city mission in Chicago. We were urged to distinguish the core of Quakerism from its cultural accretions, with the implication that a Christ-centered evangelism is a more powerful form of outreach than liberal do-gooding. I agree that Quakerism is all too often a comfortably middle-class phenomenon. I note, though, that when our meeting took the step into the Sanctuary movement, we followed the lead of Jews and Unitarians. Religious motivation doesn't always come with an orthodox label.

May 27 ▪ Thinking further on the question of religious motivation, I recalled the arguments I've had about the religious element in pastoral counseling. When others have objected to non-directive counseling as not sufficiently Christ- or God-centered, I have replied that the counselor's act of acceptance and empowering attention *is* the Christ in the situation. Secular counseling can be skewed to manipulative ends, to be sure; but that is harder to do when the counselor takes himself out of the center.

Perhaps in this time of lack of firm upbringing in moral values, it is less possible to trust in a basic moral balance-wheel in those who are counseled. Carl Rogers, who died at eighty-five this year, could have this trust because he came from a hard-working, rural, religious background. After a period of youthful missionary idealism, attending Christian student conferences, he lost his childhood faith during graduate studies, replacing it with a scientific humanism; but his experience in counseling gradually swung him back toward a faith in relationship rather than scientific techniques, and finally an openness to "New Age" thinking. This in a way was a return to religious grounding, though in an unorthodox way. I was struck with the parallels in life of the veteran peace activist E. Raymond Wilson, also a product of the rural Midwest, also feeling a youthful calling to a Christian vocation, also losing this enthusiasm during graduate study in New York. Fortunately, he learned at a conference that "faith is not belief in spite of evidence, but life in scorn of consequences." His pacifism and Quakerism have anchored his life of faith.

I expect this sort of evolutionary spiral was not uncommon in that generation. But younger persons have different backgrounds—more urban, more broken homes, religion either defensive or absent. What do they have to evolve from or return to?

May 29 ▪ I have been making a preliminary survey of the task I've set for myself this summer: straightening out the tangled subdivisions of the Quakerism books in the meeting library. Different people seem to have used different decimals, and I need to make some logical sense out of the varieties of books by and about Quakers. On the whole, I rather enjoy fitting the books into the Dewey decimal system; it is somewhat like a judge's task in finding the most relevant rule of law for the circumstances of the case before him and following precedent—in the library this is previous usage and the needs of its readers.

So I wrestle with the various shadings of Quaker subject-matter. Then I get bogged down in the odd lacunae of our haphazard card catalog and wonder how I ever got into this line of work. But on the whole I have the affection for this odd library that one might have for an eccentric old aunt whose hair is always in disarray and who can never find her glasses.

June 5 and 6 ▪ It has been perfect weather for the fiftieth reunion activities at the College. My classmates arrived, cheerful, chattering and vigorous. As I expected, I hung around in the background while everybody else greeted old friends and exchanged the shared experiences of successful over-achievers. A few shook my hand with a hearty "Glad to see you again," though I'm sure they don't remember me at all.

I looked, as Elizabeth Vining has done on similar occasions, for a "congenial mouse" with whom to converse. One such was the daughter of A.J. Muste. I also managed a word or two with a classmate who had worked in England with Michael Polanyi, a philosopher and physicist who combined both religious and scientific wisdom in his book *Personal Knowledge*. I had found this book helpful in reconciling these two ways of thinking as had my classmate Bill Scott. He hopes to write Polanyi's biography and I certainly hope to read it.

June 7 ▪ The fine weather departed with the reunion; but a number of my classmates showed up at meeting. It was then I saw the more reflective and seeking side of those who just the night before were drinking and dining with the customary reunion conviviality.

Afterwards, Bill Scott's wife Ann sought the help of our library's resources on Quaker devotional writings and we fell into discussing Christianity, Quakerism and universalism. The figure of speech occurred to me that we should all respect each others' religious roots and appreciate our several flowers. Her small and isolated meeting in Reno, Nevada, is struggling with these questions. As we talked, I discovered the Scotts know another favorite author of mine, Father William Johnston, scholar of Zen as well as Christian mysticism, a man of Irish charm and radiant love, by her account. This was for me the real reunion, one based on concinnity of spirit rather than where we went to college.

We all finally departed amid raindrops, reminiscent of the message of one classmate in meeting likening us to raindrops that merge after falling and then disappear in the ground of daily living. One of us had quoted from Shakespeare's *Henry V:* "We are but warriors of the working-day. . . . But, by the mass, our hearts are in the trim."

June 20 ▪ Reading and discussion of possible Pendle Hill pamphlets can stimulate my mind for days. This time we considered in committee two manuscripts: one declared that the sacraments of Eucharist and baptism are scripturally or-dained, while the other stated that sacraments are unscriptural. One wishes they had the courage to acknowledge their different spiritual needs—one needs the sacraments, the other doesn't—and take responsibility for their decisions.

June 22 ▪ Recently, I heard an enthusiastic account of a group get-together of single Friends. I have often observed that our suburban families, like Noah's animals who always enter the Ark two by two, plan their sociability around homes and couples, singles being odd people left out. I'm happy for those singles who seem to be finding a warm hearth, so to speak, for their often lonely and wounded spirits after divorce or bereavement. But I don't seem to need such therapy right now, partly because of my reclusive habits and partly because I already belong to a number of groups of poetry lovers, librarians and editors. I have to take care to preserve time for being creatively alone.

June 23 ▪ I am still brooding about the alarming thesis of a book by a psychology professor, Barry Schwartz, *The Battle for Human Nature*. He believes that the idea of the "economic man" acting in a free market, sociobiology studying the evolution of the "selfish gene," and B.F. Skinner's behaviorism of operant conditioning, have combined to push society down the path to conceiving of everything, including people and relationships, as so many commodities with no ulterior value of anything for its own sake. Today we read of self-proclaimed patriots enriching themselves from illicit arms deals, relationships becoming disposable when the cost-benefit analysis tips the wrong way, politicians elected by PAC money.

Ultimately, no society can cohere without moral valuation; yet science outlaws value judgments from its view of human nature. It's easier to describe the symptoms of this degenerative disease than to prescribe a remedy. Schwartz, as a Jew, has the Torah to take hold of, and we Christians can try to realize the Kingdom of God; but how about those who no longer have any such anchor to hold to? It will take more than notional education—you need a deep gut feeling that some values, such as people, are worth sacrificing for, whatever the economic calculus may dictate.

June 30 ▪ I have just returned from a three-day church

librarians' conference, held at Haverford College. What memories come back to me as I revisited places that seemed haunted by the people and activities of the Friends Conference on Religion and Psychology that used to meet here. Here by the duckpond, Teresina Havens led us in tài-chi in the mornings; there stand the venerable trees we gave ritual praise to before departing. Now I am with a different group—less artistic, less "flaky," if you will, mostly sensible middle-aged women, a few men lost among them. We bustled about from workshops to ceremonial banquets with awards and speeches and general warm enthusiasm as retiring officers were lauded for their past accomplishments and incoming officers dreamed of accomplishments to come.

At reunion time, the weather was perfect, but at the end deteriorated into the usual Delaware valley steambath. I came home to find the milk delivery I thought I had countermanded souring on my torrid doorstep. Ah, back to the real world!

July 8 ▪ Today I take time out to ponder the mysteries of life as reflected in baseball. The Phillies are a team of very able players who seem to invent innumerable ways of losing games—and then suddenly, as they did last night, win one despite their previous ineptitude.

There is drama in baseball, and as the ancient Greeks knew, there is more to drama than wins or losses; there is the strange ebb and flow of fortune that is the central mystery of human affairs. In Scripture, the stars in their courses fought against Sisera, Greek heroes wrestled with the gods as well as their own fatal flaws, Shakespeare spoke of a destiny that shapes our ends. How much of the final score is due to faith and how much to the quality of the team? Do we score a base hit for Brutus or an error on Caesar? How much of our destiny is due, in Shakespeare's words, to "a surfeit of our own behavior?" I doubt if these questions can be answered in either-or terms. As the ancient Chinese of the *I Ching* knew, we are part of a moving web of transmutations. Without a sense of inner and outer harmony, the pitcher "loses" the strike zone or gets off his rhythm, the batter gropes his way into a slump and tries too hard for a hit. Like the practitioner of meditation, the player must find the perfect mean between trying too hard and not trying enough. "Teach us to care and not to care," in T.S. Eliot's words. Baseball can thus be symbolic of life's tremendous game in which we are all players.

July 9 ▪ On the train to town, one half of my mind was on the article I was reading about the fragility of natural ecological systems and how our National Parks are destabilizing them in a well-intentioned effort to preserve them. With the other half of my mind I was noting the small and scrubby patches of tough and enduring weeds that manage to persist in the most unlikely corners of the web of railroad tracks and sidings near 30th Street Station. Perhaps, instead of mourning the death of wilderness, we might learn something from studying the survival value of these unglamorous kinds of crab-grass, ragweed, or sumac. The future evolution may lie with them.

July 11 ▪ Two discoveries today—two sides of Mother Nature: the fierce and the gentle. A long line of shredded bark on the trunk of the old cucumber tree by the front entrance showed that it had been struck by lightening in the storm that roared up two nights ago. I had heard the characteristic dry snap simultaneously with the lightning flash, and knew it had struck nearby (we have had two trees struck in previous years); but I hadn't located the damage until now.

After inspecting the wounded tree, I passed close to an azalea bush beside the street and noticed a robin fluttering in protest overhead. I then saw half hidden in the bush a nest with the quivering, up-thrust necks of three nestlings within.

There have been other wildlife dramas through the years. We have lost most of the pine tees that harbored a colony of grackles which arrived promptly on Washington's Birthday (when this was a fixed date) and I no longer have to defend my garbage can from the raccoon who raised her young in a spare chimney of this old house; but I still see a rabbit nibbling the grass in the mornings.

July 15 ▪ The journal of a quiet life runs to trivia. How trivial should a diarist get? I am encouraged by such a passage as this from the English novelist Barbara Pym's diary *A Very Private Eye:* "We discussed the technique of misery on the way back, then had tea in the kitchen. In the afternoon I washed my hair and parted it in the middle again." Misery and tea are well intertwined in life.

My own trivia today combines a beautifully cool and inviting day with the fact that my telephone line is out of order and I have had to waste the day awaiting a repair man who never came. A small cloud of anger and frustration hangs over my head.

July 16 ▪ Now I am connected to the world again. My telephone is behaving properly and the repair man could find nothing wrong. I felt helpless without a phone as I have felt helpless without the use of a car. Of course, people lived for centuries without these things, but other arrangements were in place—messenger boys or interurban trolleys. But once introduced, new technology shapes society so as to make itself indispensable. This new shaping renders obsolete the old way of thinking that conceives of isolating and altering individual factors in an experiment while leaving the others unchanged. Now ecologists, for example, are teaching us that to change or add one factor is to transform the whole. And before the ecologists, the mystics knew that we are part of a seamless web, part of what Eastern philosophers call Indra's net.

Well, today a new factor entered the cosmic net—the land-lord's wife has presented him with a baby daughter.

July 18 ▪ I was shown the new baby—a tiny, sleepy bundle. I have never had the longing to have a baby, nor would I wish to have the daily (and nightly) care of one; but I do enjoy the gentle, cuddling contact with a being who still possesses the Edenic wholeness of mind with body. I am glad I have known and played with a few babies in my lifetime. Everyone should have a chance to know and enjoy a baby.

July 24 ▪ Waiting while my car was inspected, I kept my mind occupied with the delicate comedy of a Barbara Pym novel while my body melted in the ninety-degree heat of the service station. The novel describes the incidents of a Church of England parish life—a life of dowdy old ladies and smooth young curates balancing tea-cups. I don't know whether Barbara Pym found something deeper in church-going than a mild antiquarian hobby; perhaps it was only in observing the trivia of parish doings that she could glimpse the unrealized promise of community offered to the reticent English parishioners.

Then I returned home to read psychiatrist Scott Peck's urgent plea, in *The Different Drum,* for generating true community, so lacking in the churches as well as in society at large. If Christians really became open to community life based on love, the temples of Mammon would begin to crumble, he believes; but it would require commitment and possible martyrdom on the part of the comfy churchgoers in the congregation.

I wondered about us Quakers, balanced between tepidity and transformation. I hope we will be more than the subject of gentle Jane Austen-ish stories of old Quaker ways; yet, we don't seem likely to be George Foxes shaking the earth for ten miles round. Perhaps our quiet insistence on Light-gathered consensus and mediation will keep a gentle revolution going.

And now I must gather things for our Jumble Sale.

August 7 ▪ I'm reading Barbara Pym's *Quartet in Autumn,* about four lonely single people about to retire from their humdrum jobs, quietly withering away from loneliness: a sad book, but with wry humor. One friend, rather condescending, is "unwilling to give up the luxury of having a friend less useful than herself." These people, two men and two women, find it difficult to break out of their British reserve to need or be needed by others. One of the women, a true eccentric fighting off well-meaning attempts at helpfulness, reminds me of my late eccentric aunt.

This gray, depressing unconnectedness is the end result of a society which has forgotten the art of community. It pervades the poetry of Philip Larkin, a friendly correspondent of Barbara Pym's. And it fills most of the recent short stories I've read in the *Atlantic.*

Recently I've had a few pleasant notes from the old members I've sent birthday cards to. So perhaps even this mild gesture serves as a connection in this world of encapsulated loners.

August 31 ▪ Two TV programs back to back this evening told the story of two different vanishing species—the California condors and the Shakers. The modern world has less and less room in its crowded society for such large, slow-breeding birds or for celibate contemplatives creating buildings and furniture for love of perfection, not for the bottom line. Celibacy has little survival value today, but one hopes those who venture in the spiritual life will not forget the value of sublimation in directing our energy toward the hallowing of all our lives.

September 1 ▪ This year of the Constitution is a good time to contemplate the myths—the "sacred history," as it were—

which people create to engender a sense of nationhood.

Religious movements, of course, also have their sacred history, from the Jews' exodus, their kings and prophets, exile and ingathering in Israel, to our Quaker history of George Fox in his leather breeches.

How true are these pictures and are they necessary? Their truth lies less in history than in their aspirations for the future—what we wish we were. But we cannot embody them until we acknowledge the shadow side of our shortcomings and go on from there. So, let our lives speak, in the land of the free and the home of the brave!

September 12 ▪ I've attended a peace rally outside the National Guard Armory in nearby Media, protesting the use of the Guard in the covert war against Nicaragua. Present on this gray morning were the usual kind-faced veteran Quakers, enthusiastic college girls and scrawny youngsters with fledgling beards. Bathed in a sense of our righteousness, we listened to peptalks that told us what we wanted to hear, even as President Reagan is told only what he wants to hear. Beyond raising our own spirits I'm not sure what difference these occasions make. Behind us, the town of Media pursued its usual occupations. Anyway, we had better luck with the weather than the visiting Pope did in rainy Miami.

September 18 ▪ Is it far-fetched to liken the thought that goes into a major purchase to a certain kind of prayer? Those whose prayer is the expression of the "soul's sincere desire" describe a process of honest expression of need in dialogue with the intuition of divine requirements until the two coincide. Similarly, I find the approach to a purchase requires the definition of what it is one truly wants and this is shaped in turn by what is available and affordable.

I have been unhappy with my present typing facilities. What

was it I needed—a word processor? That would be excessive. Something more than the electric typewriter I had, but something less than full processing. In any case, my first processing is done by a pencil with a good eraser. A morning spent at Sears trying out electronic typewriters helped me to zero in on a portable machine with enough memory and correction ability to meet the needs of those tedious jobs of making catalog cards and typing the minutes of the meeting. I think I shall do these tasks more cheerfully.

October 3 ▪ While the first chill rain of autumn is dashing at the windows and while I was preparing a program of the poetry of Vachel Lindsay, I think of the unexpected discovery that an elderly member of our meeting knew Lindsay's sister, had visited his hometown of Springfield, Illinois, and had taken a walking trip following Lindsay's itinerary along the Santa Fe trail. This was in the 1940s, and the photographs this latter-day pilgrim had taken show the old West of mule teams and lonely railroad depots little changed since Lindsay's days. Surely all is changed now to mechanized farms and roaring superhighways. My friend had met people who knew Lindsay and were still bitter about the presumed causes of his suicide. This rainy morning was well spent in making this past life live again through the transmission of memories.

October 12 ▪ I have survived that annual convulsion of our meeting known as the Jumble Sale. After several afternoons in the basement sorting cartons of old books for sale, I am vividly reminded how many dull or worthless books have lurked until now in dusty closets, and how soon they make one's back ache.

October 18 ▪ I've been cataloging a new book by a member of our meeting—how swiftly my new typewriter's memory rattled off the card set! Is this joy akin to that of answered prayer?

The book's author is very much opposed to the "supernatural" element in religion and would put religion on a naturalistic basis. I would have thought that battle with the "old-time religion" had been over long ago, but the resurgence of fundamentalism shows that the issue is still relevant. Yet a purely naturalistic religion is one-sided. The mischief began when Protestantism neglected or abandoned the sense of immanence or incarnation of the divine in the natural. Catholicism still retains this sense, thanks to its mystical element. Religion pertains to what is more fundamental than nature; nature manifests it and at the same time is judged by it.

Sometimes I tinker with expressing the basis of religion as briefly and simply as possible. Here is one attempt: the nature of God is expressed in the Biblical self-description —"I am that I am." Of the natural world, as Charles Williams has said, "This also is Thou; neither is this Thou"—a paradox similar to the odd Zen question: Does a dog have the Buddha Nature?

Religion should not be put into propositions or argued about. The proper expression of its truths is in stories and parables like those of the Sufi, Zen Buddhists, Hasids, and especially Jesus. These parables make no explicit statements, but hand you a hunk of reality with the implication: "Those that have ears, let them hear."

October 25 ▪ Someone in worship today gave a brief summary of the naturalistic interpretation of religion. How rational, judicious and powerless seemed our intellectual expressions and how little they met the need of a young attender, obviously in need of deeper ministry, who left, overcome by emotion, in the middle of meeting. The real ministry of our meeting came from the concern of several who followed him out to give him comfort. I saw that such lovingkindness, call it love or agape, is the manifestation in the natural world of that which transcends it. Love does have power—not the political or mechanical power the world seems to covet, but a basic power that works in another way, not by overcoming but by reunion. Such a working, when it points to its source, can be called a miracle—not a breach of nature, but an inbreak of love.

I should add to the basic religious statement I made a few days ago that the "I am that I am" is manifested as love of this powerful/powerless sort and is known only by participation.

Before I could gather these thoughts together, the meeting came to its close. Going home, I mused on the occasional tensions in our meeting between its rational-academic and its quietly religious tendencies. Sometimes the balance tips one way, sometimes the other. At times, a few members have fallen away to worship in more congenial, more "spiritual" meetings; this is a pity, for a secularized meeting needs a religious few to leaven the lump, just as a more religiously enthusiastic meeting needs a few good agnostics as burrs under its saddle.

Sometimes I have felt very much in the minority; but as a religiously-minded intellectual, I hope to remain as a kind of bridge between the two tendencies in the meeting's life, presenting material in our library that might question and deepen both ways of thinking.

October 31 ▪ I have been asked to lead an adult forum in January and already ideas are coming together round the topic in my mind like iron filings to a magnet or—to change the simile—like corals and other sea creatures fastening themselves to the framework of a sunken ship while strange fish swim in and out of its crevices, looking for shelter.

It occurs to me that this is the opposite of that kind of meditation which clears the mind of thoughts, becoming a still mirror for the Light to shine on. I love the idea of meditation, but can't empty my mind. When, however, I swim in the mental sea of rich coral growths and multiplying associations,

I seem to have found my native element. So be it.

November 4 ▪ At a session of the Visiting Committee I became acquainted with the context of those birthday cards I sent out. Visits are paid to many of the old or infirm and an unobtrusive eye is kept on the welfare of all the meeting membership. This is the quiet networking that keeps community alive, and it is the older women who do it. Here is the balance to the more academic side of our meeting.

Later, I thought back to my half-forgotten courses in pastoral care at Massachusetts General Hospital. I recalled the advantage clergy have in being the one kind of helping professional who can take the initiative in offering counsel; and also the besetting sin the clergy have in being too ready with theology in a situation that calls for a listening relationship. Our situation is the reverse: we are too respectably middle-class to intrude on the troubles of others unasked, nor do we feel qualified to tackle the big religious questions. We can offer a kindly presence and that is often enough; but have we not lost that sense the earlier Friends had of being spoken through that gave them the authority to speak to someone's condition in what they called a "religious opportunity"?

November 26 ▪ A feast day like Thanksgiving is an embarrassment to a family-less person like myself. This time I was invited to dinner with a neighboring couple whose children live far away and who usually share their feast with sojourning foreign students or others at loose ends. Apparently, none of these was available except myself, so the three of us shared the meal and a peaceful evening by the fireplace afterward.

December 1 ▪ I'm glad to find that my display of library books does spark some lively conversation at our coffee hour. Last Sunday it ranged from need for community to the future of the Society of Friends. One of our more scholarly members wondered where the next generation of dynamic Quakers was going to come from, noting that many liberal Friends are refugees from evangelical backgrounds running on the nearly exhausted momentum of an inherited sense of mission.

Last evening, I went to a lecture by Douglas Gwyn, himself a Foxian scholar, who seems to have resewn his academic robes to be a "born again" Quaker who has had an overwhelming conversion experience similar to Fox's. He spoke in measured, worshipful tones of Fox's illumined life, ending with James Nayler's dying words. During the silent worship that followed, one speaker quietly reminded us that each must look for his/her own way to the Light within, and another sang a spontaneous song to the Love that uplifts.

We probably need both the warm enthusiasm and the cool disillusion embodied in these scholars to find our way between the skeptical and the religious.

December 5 ▪ I have been struggling with composing the minutes of yesterday's Pendle Hill Publications meeting. Our discussions are long and absorbing: always there are lively agreements and disagreements about the manuscripts up for judgment and now there are venturesome business decisions to be made about expansion into book publishing and cooperation with other Quaker publishers which strain my recording capacity to the limit. I confess that after forty years I'm still in awe of the articulateness and expertise of the various committee members I have known. I am now a kind of oldest inhabitant. This has been my most interesting committee, with more genuine results than others I've been on which so often become make-work sessions threshing old straw year after year.

December 6 ▪ This morning an architect showed slides to illustrate his forum talk on spiritual values in architecture. He began with citing the natural piety of the ancient Chinese, who revered the character of wood, stone, metal and water. Then a succession of slides showing buildings in their settings, from plain Vermont barns to Chartres Cathedral, even including a jigsaw ornament on our old railroad station and the way the rafters intersect under the roof of our meetinghouse porch. This re-sensitized my eye for the structural details I had taken snapshots of in years past, from doorways of old New England houses to the wrought ironwork in Charleston, South Carolina.

Our speaker told a Zen story of how a tantalizing glimpse of the sea is more memorable than an ever-present panorama. So in these brief glimpses of beauty—human beings cooperating with nature—one may, like Wordsworth, "see into the life of things."

On the eve of my seventy-first birthday, my first year of being seventy rounds to a close. It has been a kind year to me and I wouldn't mind cloning it for several more years before time takes its inevitable toll. It ends hopefully with the Reagan-Gorbachev summit. I've heard it said that the economics of both countries require an end to the Cold War. I hope it is so.

Looking back on what I have recorded, many of my reflections seem like small snippets of opinions, like the Yankee habit of saving pieces of string too short to save. But it is a reflection of what has been going on in my mind and trivial as it may seem, my life is still interesting. I can only hope to trudge onward, albeit a bit creakier in the joints but still "in the trim," and my message for the Angel of Death is: Don't interrupt me!

Background Reading

Bacon, Margaret Hope. *Let This Life Speak: The Legacy of Henry Joel Cadbury*. University of Pennsylvania Press, 1987.

Dickson, Paul. *The Library in America*. Facts on File Publications, c. 1986.

Dinesin, Isak. "A Consolatory Tale" in *Winter's Tales*. Random House, c.1942.

Furlong, Monica. *Zen Effects: The Life of Alan Watts*. Random House, 1972.

Goodwin, Doris Kearns. *The Fitzgeralds and the Kennedys*. Simon & Schuster, 1987.

Kirschenbaum, Howard. *On Becoming Carl Rogers*. Delta paperback, 1980.

Larkin, Philip. *High Windows*. Straus & Giroux, 1974.
    The Whitsun Wedding. Faber & Faber, 1964.

Le Guin, Ursula. *The Wizard of Earthsea*. Parnassus, 1968.

Luke, Mary and Ellen Luke. *Teilhard: The Man, The Priest, The Scientist*. Doubleday, 1977.

Newman, Daisy. *A Golden String*. Harper and Row, 1987.

O'Connor, Flannery. *A Good Man is Hard to Find*. Harcourt, Brace, Jovanovich, 1955.

Peck, M. Scott. *The Different Drum*. Simon & Schuster, 1987.

Pym, Barbara. *A Glass of Blessings*. Dutton, 1980.
    Quartet in Autumn. Dutton, 1978.
    A Very Private Eye. Dutton, 1974.

Sarton, May. *The Magnificent Spinster*. Norton, 1985.
    At Seventy. Norton, 1978.
    World of Light. Norton, 1976.

Schwartz, Barry. *The Battle for Human Nature*. Norton, 1986.

Vining, Elizabeth Gray. *Being Seventy*. Viking, 1978.

Watts, Alan. *In My Own Way*. Random House, Pantheon Books, 1972.

Wilson, E. Raymond. *Thus Far On My Journey*. Friends United Press, 1976.

Pendle Hill

PENDLE HILL is a residential study center and a retreat and conference center as well as the publisher of Pendle Hill books and pamphlets. It is a center for the nurture of religious life and an adult school for intensive study in those fields which help unfold the meaning of life. At Pendle Hill education is thought of in its broadest sense—the transforming of persons and society.

Pendle Hill offers a three term **residential program** from October to June. 35 to 40 persons, ranging in age from 19 to 75, enroll as students for one or more terms, joining the resident staff and families. About half the community are Friends. Among the rest a wide variety of faiths, philosophies, and cultural backgrounds is represented. Students pursue interests and concerns through study, reading, writing, meditation, dialogue, and creative projects. Each morning residents gather in **meeting for worship,** held after the manner of Friends. Pendle Hill offers five or six **courses** in the area of Quakerism, Bible, religious thought, peace and social concerns, literature and the arts, and crafts. Every student participates in the **work program,** helping with the upkeep of house and grounds and with food preparation and meal clean-up.

Admission to Pendle Hill is based upon the applicant's commitment to learning, openness to exploring religious reality, and readiness to take a responsible part in the common life of Pendle Hill. Limited **financial aid** is available for applicants unable to pay the full fees.

Pendle Hill also offers a full program of short term events through its **Extension Program:** weekend conferences and retreats; summer workshops, conferences, and retreats; a series of Monday Evening Lectures; weekly extension courses for persons not living at Pendle Hill. Persons wishing a short term experience in the resident community may also apply to be **sojourners** during most of the year.

Further details on dates and fees for all programs are available from **Pendle Hill, Wallingford, PA 19086. 215-566-4507.**

Why Pamphlets?

One of the basic ideas concerning Pendle Hill is the application of the tenets of the Society of Friends to adult education as a preparation for usefulness in the fields of religion and social action. Because it is a Quaker institution, Pendle Hill differs radically from a theological seminary or a school for social workers. As in the case of other vital movements, small or large, the idea motivating this experiment seeks embodiment in pamphlets. Pendle Hill pamphlets, like the early Christian or the early Quaker tracts, present a variety of points of view, but they are all in some way derived from another fundamental idea. Variety is evidence of life; cold uniformity presages death.

But why pamphlets? Why not more books, or magazine articles, or posters? The typical pamphlet has certain characteristics which make it an apt vehicle for experimental thought. It should be the right length to be read easily at a single sitting (9,000 words). It should portray a single thesis without wandering from it. It must be concerned with a topic of contemporary (though not necessarily topical) importance. And a Quaker pamphlet, like a Quaker sermon, must embody a concern.

Though these qualifications have never been used as a systematic check list by our Publications Committee in choosing manuscripts, they have generally applied to the 286 pamphlets we have issued since Vincent Nicholson's *Cooperation and Coercion as Methods of Social Change* began our series in 1934. Some of these pamphlets have been written by persons who have lived and worked at Pendle Hill as students and staff or who have attended conferences or visited as sojourners. Others come from a wider community of seekers.

To date, approximately 80 pamphlets are still in print. Those older pamphlets which have gone out of print are available in photocopied form. A complete list is available from the Pendle Hill bookstore.

If you are unfamiliar with Pendle Hill publications, why not start a subscription?

Order Form

Yes, please send me a subscription to Pendle Hill Pamphlets.

NAME ____

ADDRESS ____

CITY __________________ STATE _____ ZIP ___________

One year (6 issues) $10.00 ________
Two years (12 issues) 19.00 ________
Three years (18 issues) 27.00 ________

Please send a gift subscription to:

NAME ____

ADDRESS ____

CITY __________________ STATE _____ ZIP ___________

One year (6 issues) $10.00 ________
Two years (12 issues) 19.00 ________
Three years (18 issues) 27.00 ________

GIFT CARD FROM _____________________________________

ENCLOSED $ ________